FOSSILS UNCOVERED!

AN EGG THIEF?

OVIRAPTOR DISCOVERY

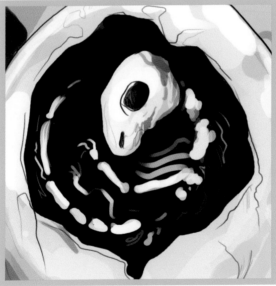

By Sarah Eason

Illustrated by Ludovic Sallé

BEARPORT
PUBLISHING

Minneapolis, Minnesota

Credits: 20b, © Ton Bangkeaw/Shutterstock; 21t, © Ozja/Shutterstock; 21b, © Audrey M. Horn/Wikimedia Commons; 22l, © Kriengsak Wiriyakrieng/ Shutterstock; 22r, © Microgen/Shutterstock; 23b, © LegART/Shutterstock.

Editor: Jennifer Sanderson
Proofreader: Harriet McGregor
Designer: Paul Myerscough
Picture Researcher: Rachel Blount

DISCLAIMER: This graphic story is a dramatization based on true events. It is intended to give the reader a sense of the narrative rather than a presentation of actual details as they occurred.

Library of Congress Cataloging-in-Publication Data

Names: Eason, Sarah, author. | Salle, Ludovic, 1985- illustrator.
Title: An egg thief? : oviraptor discovery / by Sarah Eason ; illustrated
  by Ludovic Salle.
Description: Bear claw books. | Minneapolis : Bearport Publishing Company,
  [2022] | Series: Fossils uncovered! | Includes index.
Identifiers: LCCN 2021030942 (print) | LCCN 2021030943 (ebook) | ISBN
  9781636913360 (library binding) | ISBN 9781636913438 (paperback) | ISBN
  9781636913506 (ebook)
Subjects: LCSH: Dinosaurs--Eggs--Juvenile literature. |
  Oviraptor--Behavior--Juvenile literature.
Classification: LCC QE861.6.E35 E27 2022 (print) | LCC QE861.6.E35
  (ebook) | DDC 567.912--dc23
LC record available at https://lccn.loc.gov/2021030942
LC ebook record available at https://lccn.loc.gov/2021030943

Copyright © 2022 Bearport Publishing Company. All rights reserved. No part of this publication may be reproduced in whole or in part, stored in any retrieval system, or transmitted in any form or by any means, electronic, mechanical, photocopying, recording, or otherwise, without written permission from the publisher.

For more information, write to Bearport Publishing, 5357 Penn Avenue South, Minneapolis, MN 55419. Printed in the United States of America.

CONTENTS

CHAPTER I

DESERT DISCOVERY

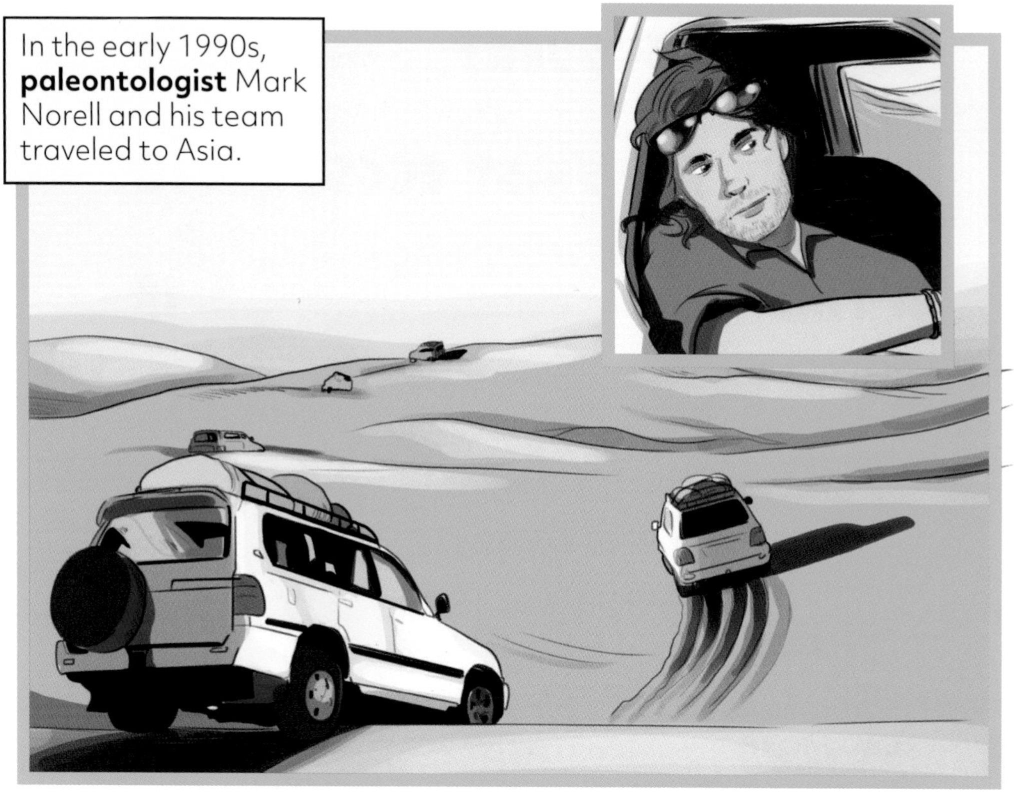
In the early 1990s, **paleontologist** Mark Norell and his team traveled to Asia.

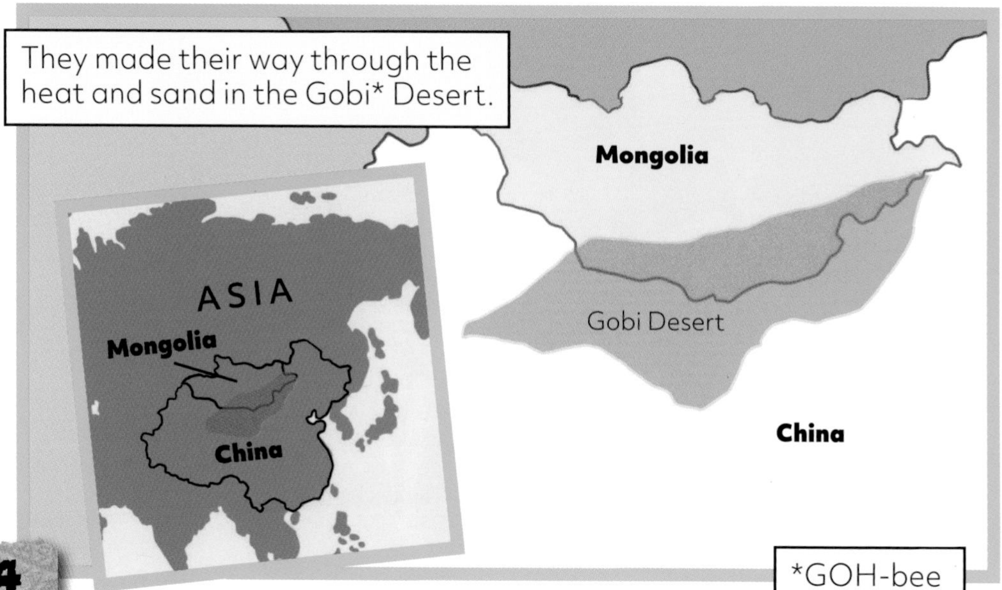
They made their way through the heat and sand in the Gobi* Desert.
Mongolia
Gobi Desert
China
ASIA
Mongolia
China
*GOH-bee

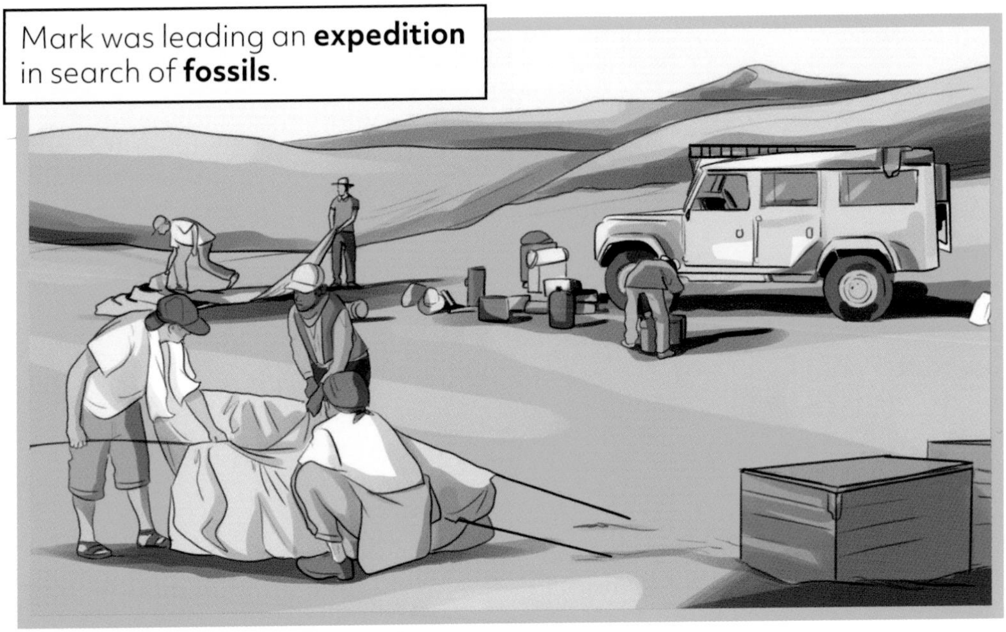
Mark was leading an **expedition** in search of **fossils**.

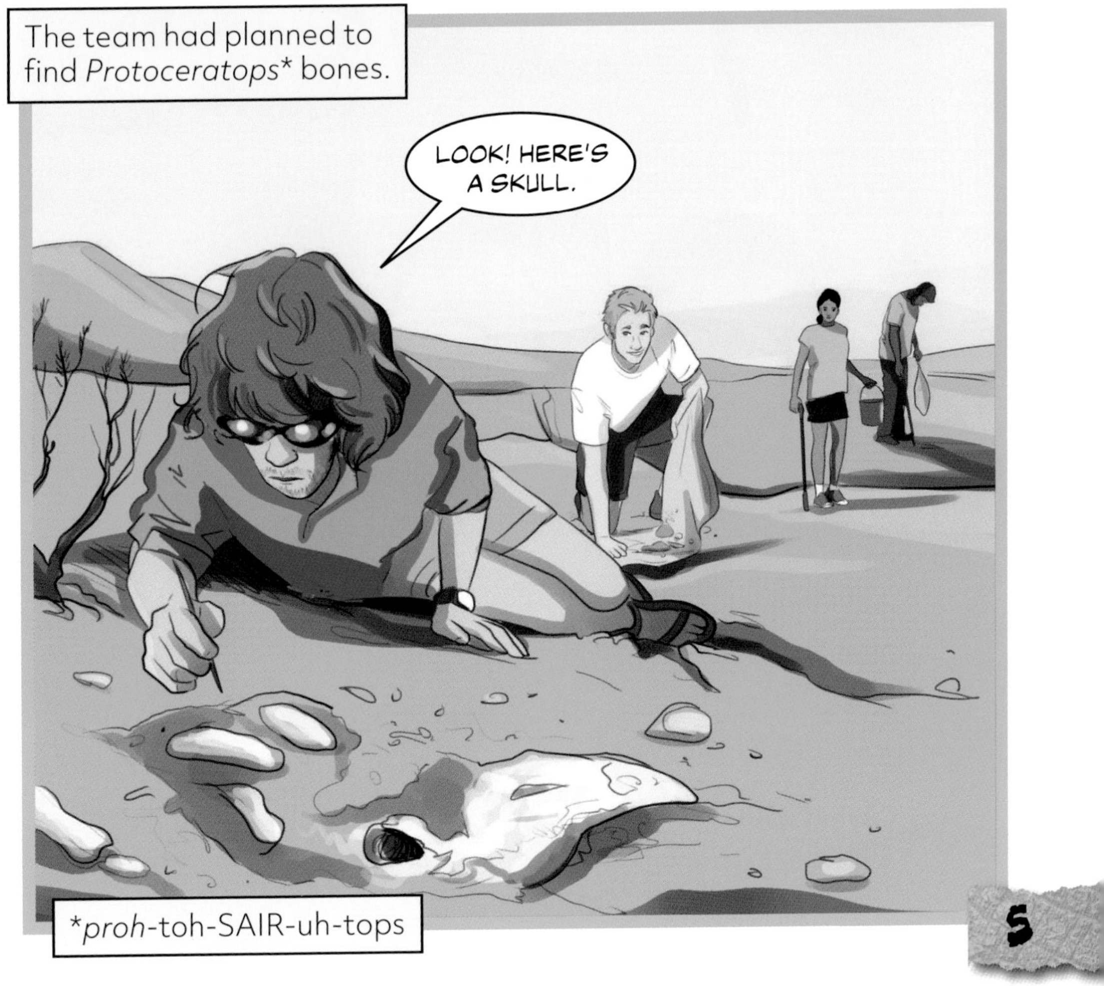
The team had planned to find *Protoceratops** bones.
LOOK! HERE'S A SKULL.
**proh*-toh-SAIR-uh-tops

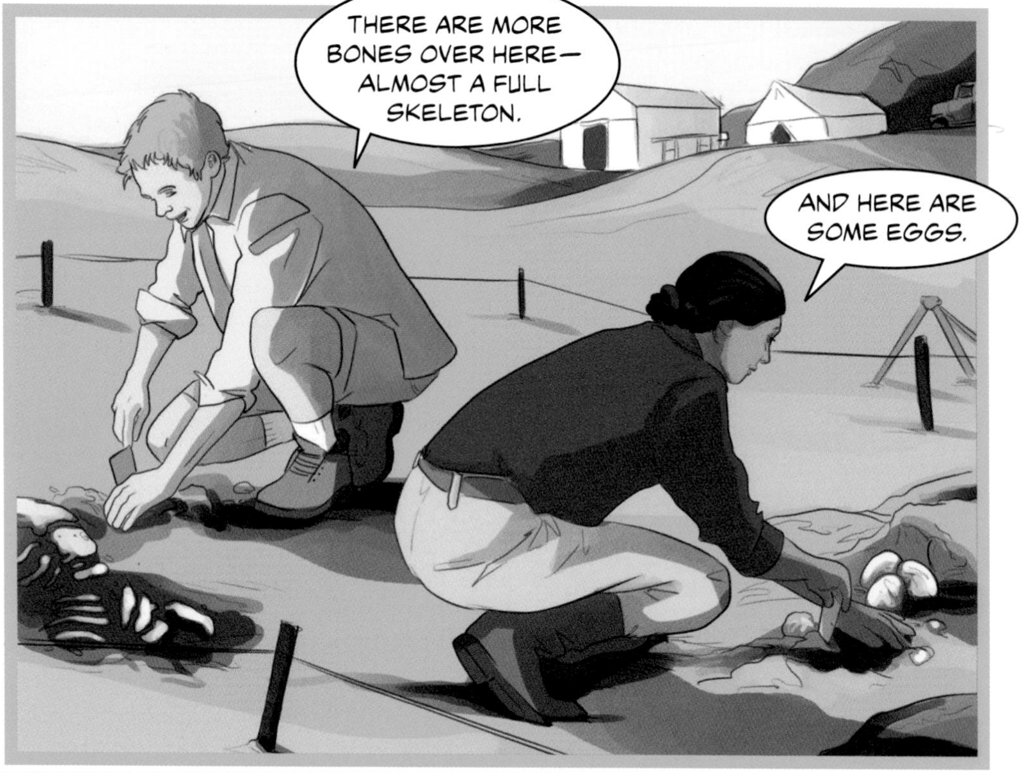
THERE ARE MORE BONES OVER HERE— ALMOST A FULL SKELETON.
AND HERE ARE SOME EGGS.

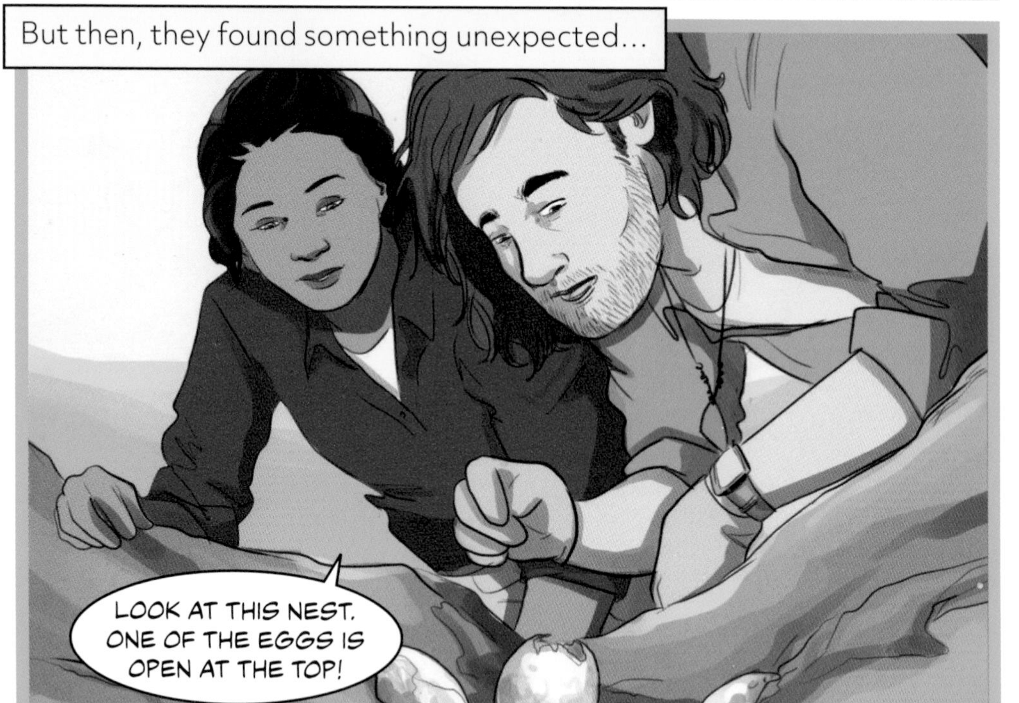
But then, they found something unexpected...
LOOK AT THIS NEST. ONE OF THE EGGS IS OPEN AT THE TOP!

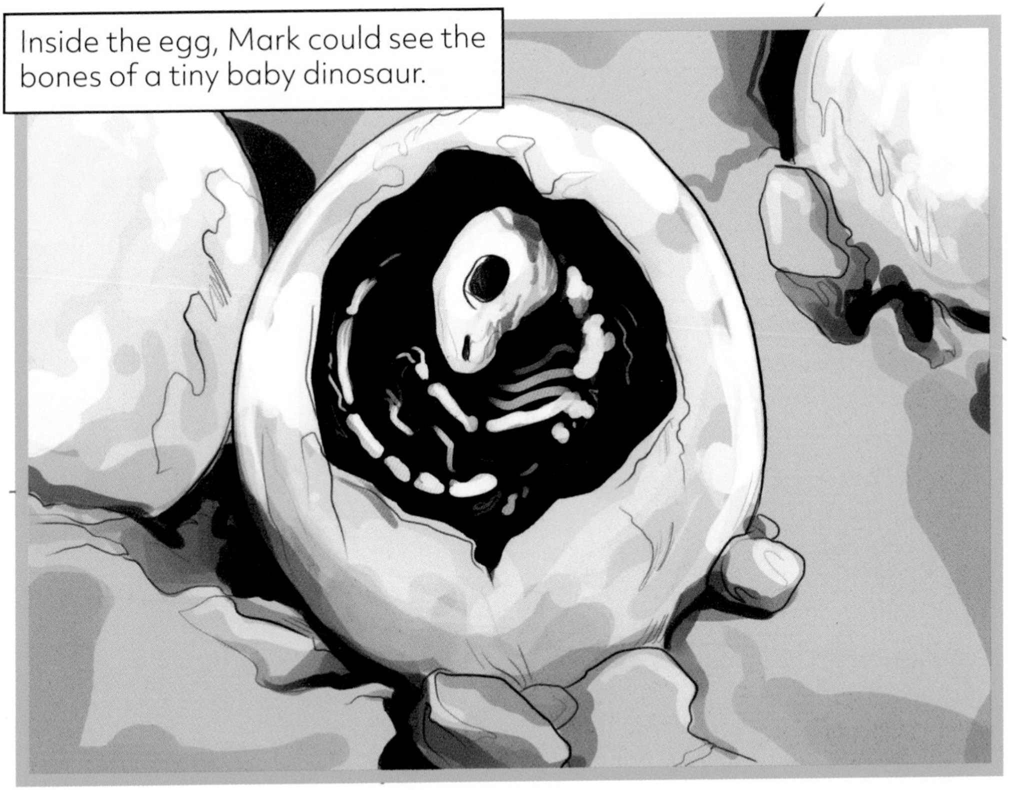
Inside the egg, Mark could see the bones of a tiny baby dinosaur.

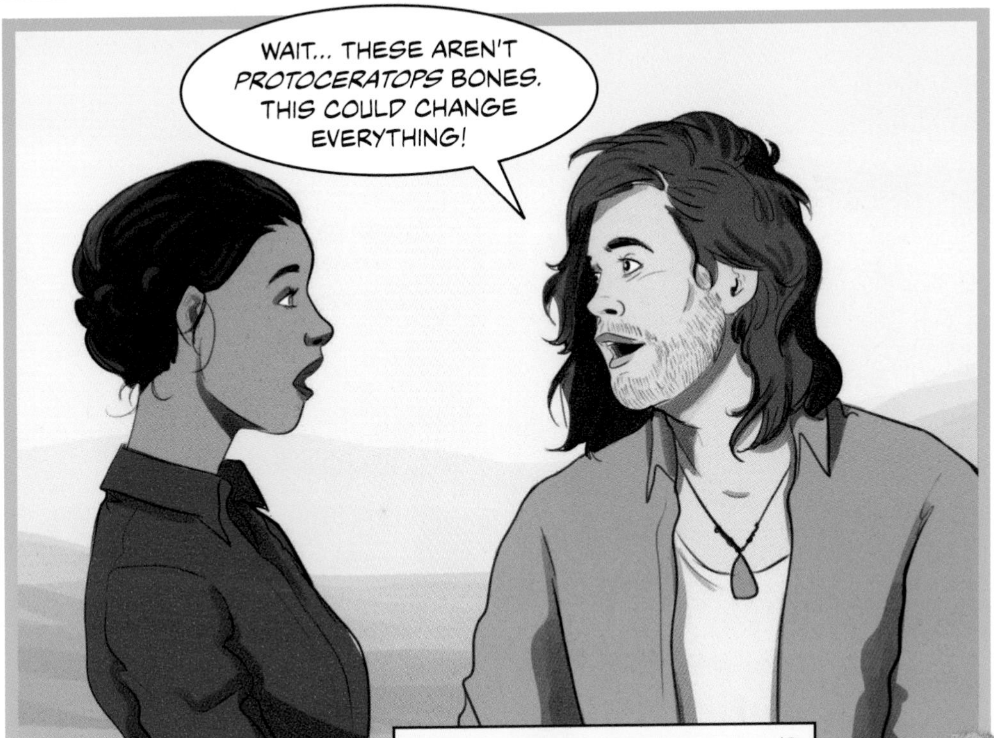
WAIT... THESE AREN'T *PROTOCERATOPS* BONES. THIS COULD CHANGE EVERYTHING!
Why was Mark so surprised?

CHAPTER 2

FINDING THE FIRST EGGS

In 1922, Roy Chapman Andrews had also led a team of paleontologists to the Gobi Desert. They were looking for **remains** of the first humans.

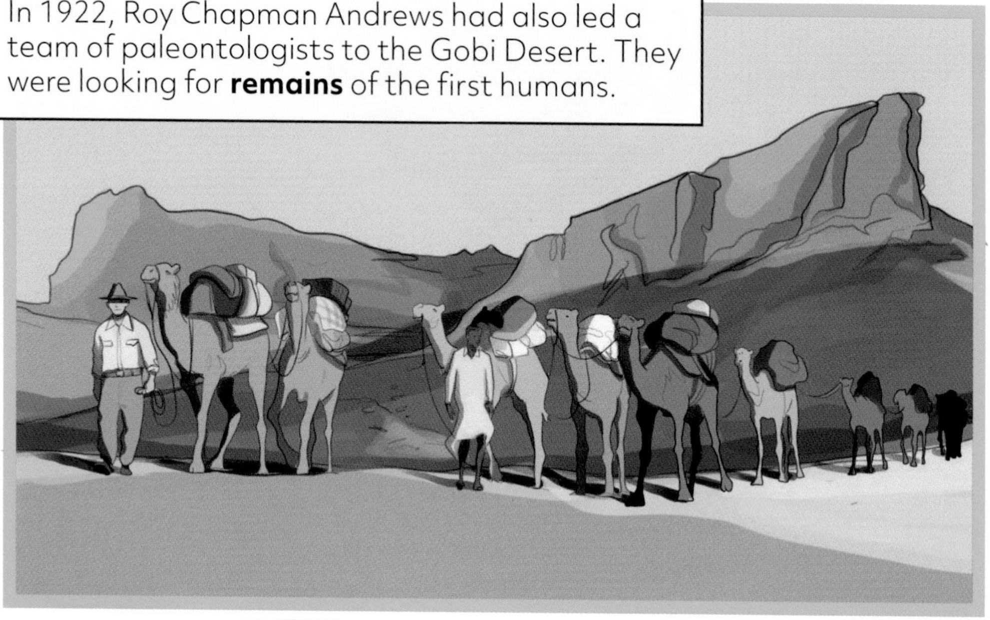

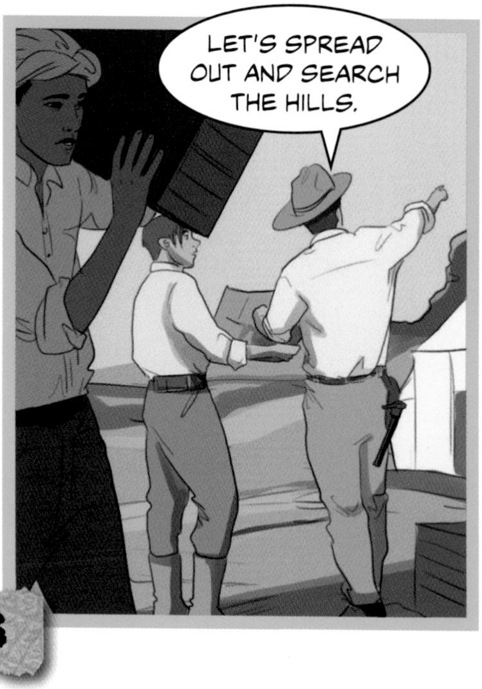
LET'S SPREAD OUT AND SEARCH THE HILLS.

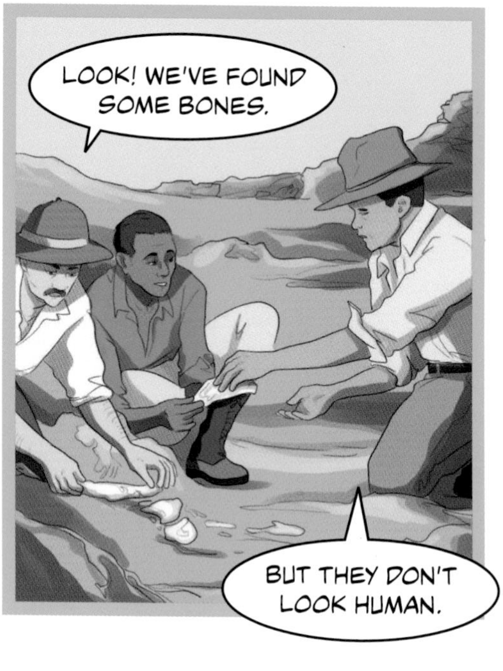
LOOK! WE'VE FOUND SOME BONES.
BUT THEY DON'T LOOK HUMAN.

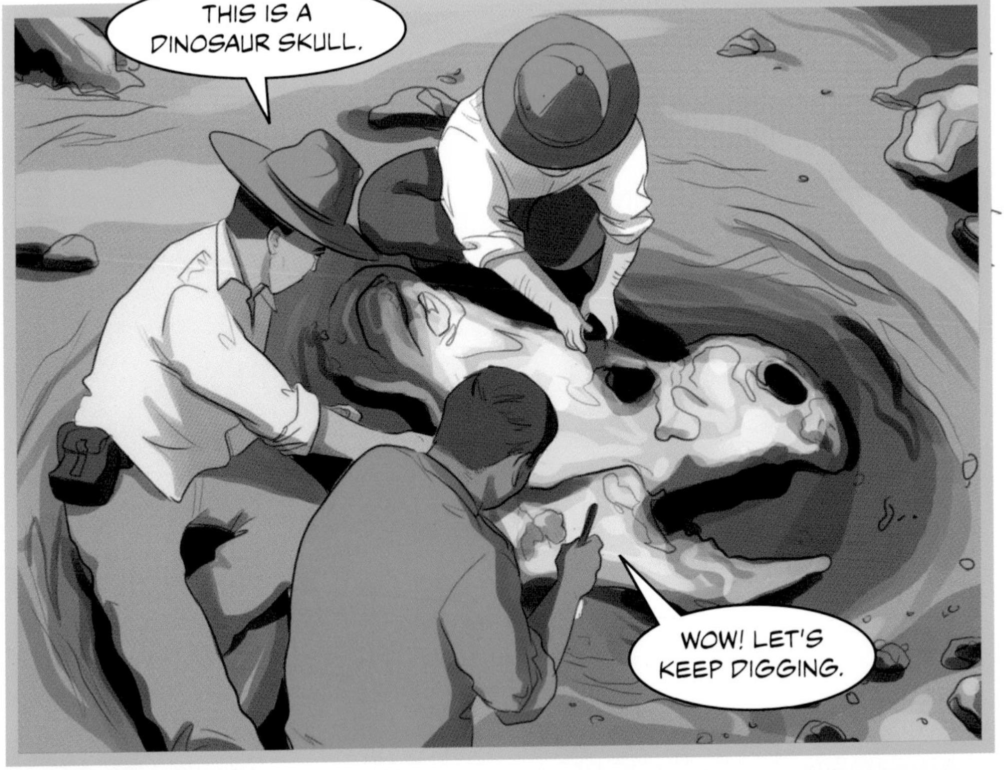
THIS IS A DINOSAUR SKULL.
WOW! LET'S KEEP DIGGING.

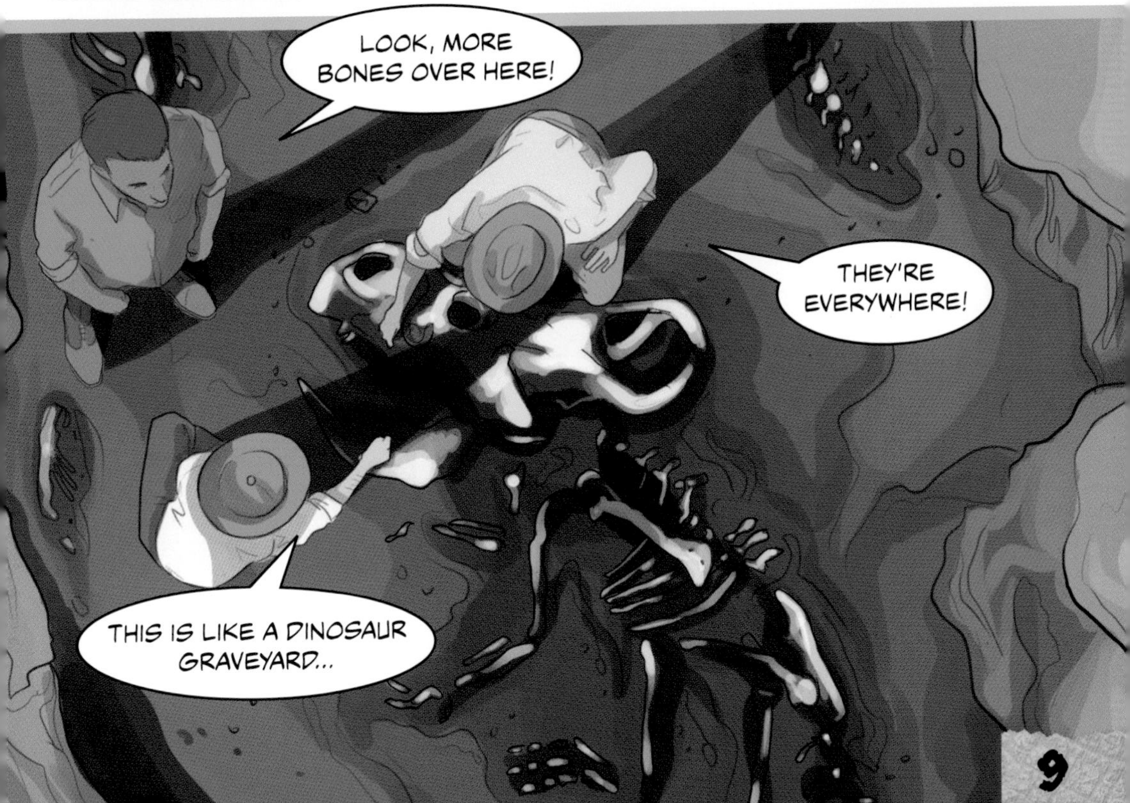
LOOK, MORE BONES OVER HERE!
THEY'RE EVERYWHERE!
THIS IS LIKE A DINOSAUR GRAVEYARD...

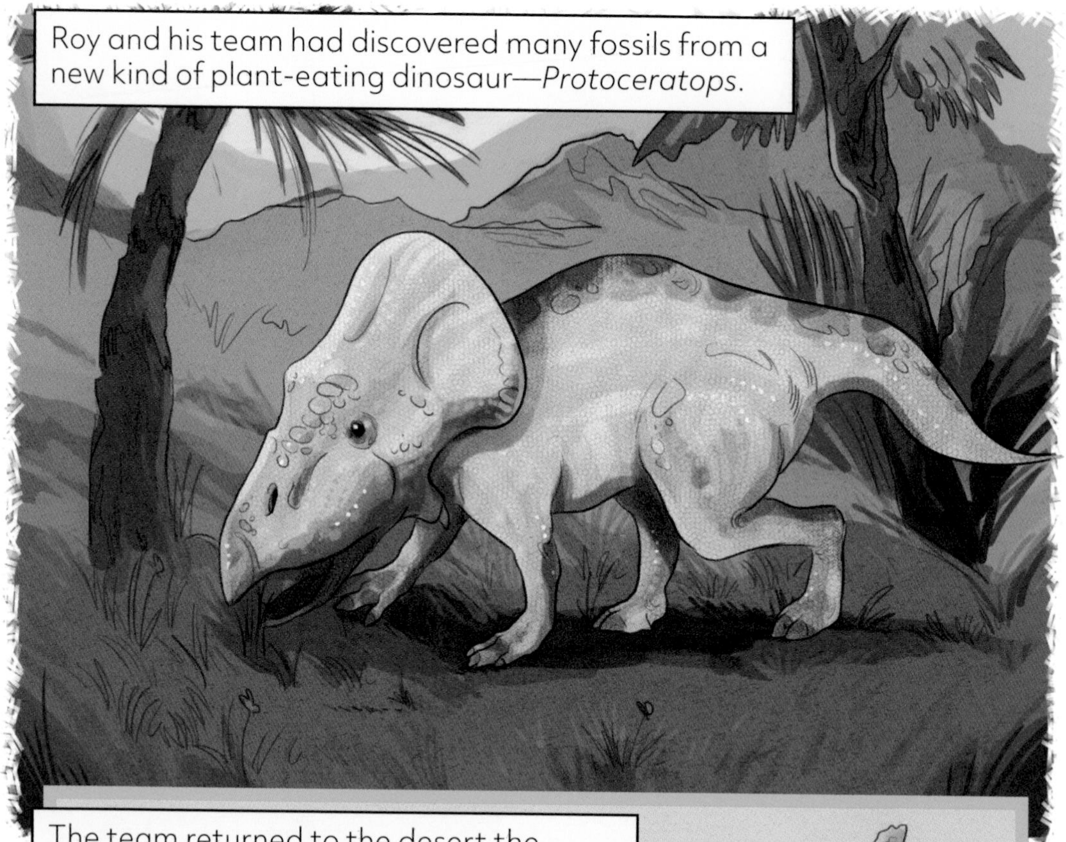
Roy and his team had discovered many fossils from a new kind of plant-eating dinosaur—*Protoceratops*.

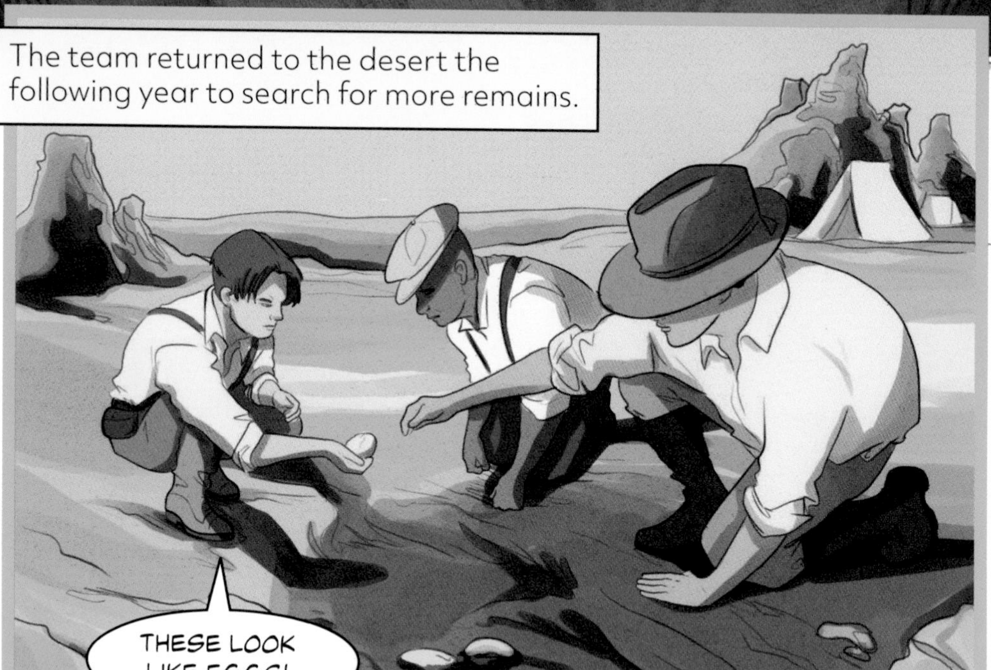
The team returned to the desert the following year to search for more remains.
THESE LOOK LIKE EGGS!

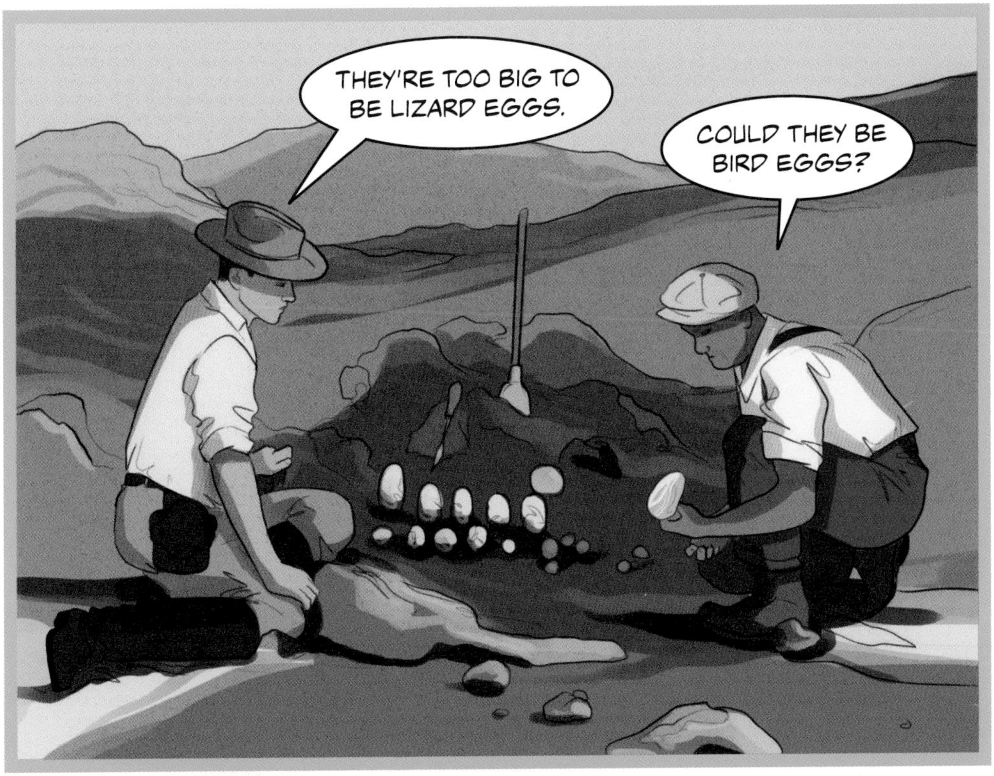
THEY'RE TOO BIG TO BE LIZARD EGGS.
COULD THEY BE BIRD EGGS?

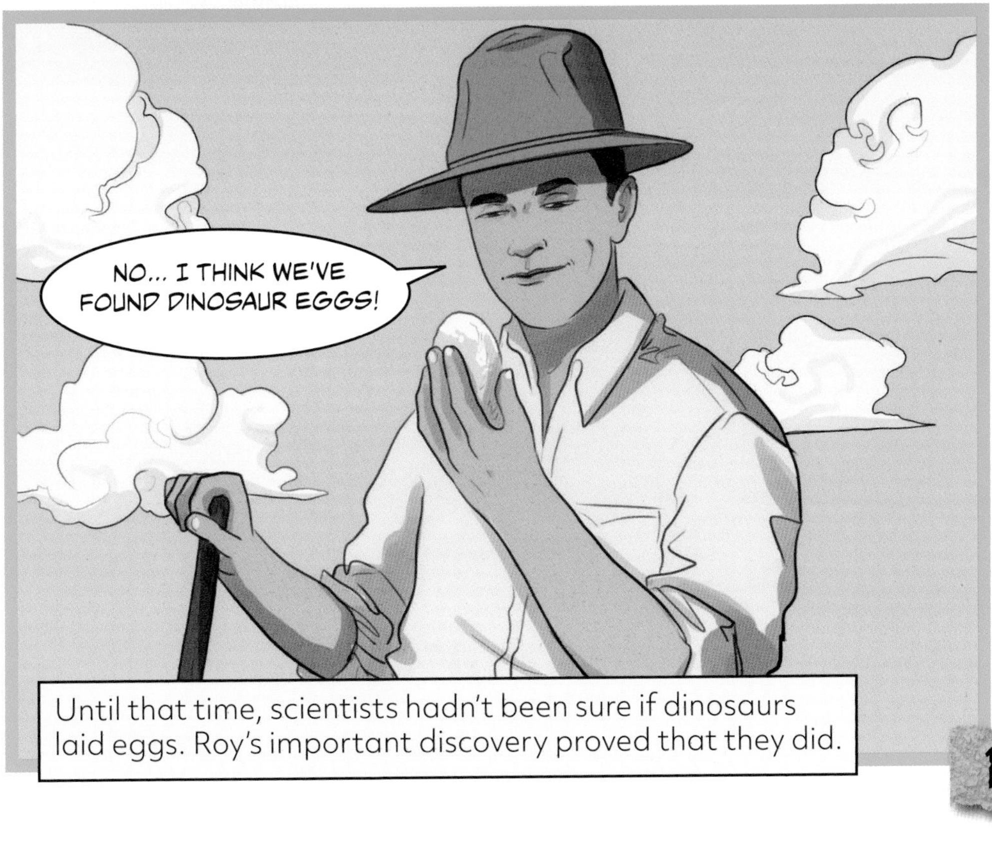
NO... I THINK WE'VE FOUND DINOSAUR EGGS!
Until that time, scientists hadn't been sure if dinosaurs laid eggs. Roy's important discovery proved that they did.

CHAPTER 3

A THIEF?

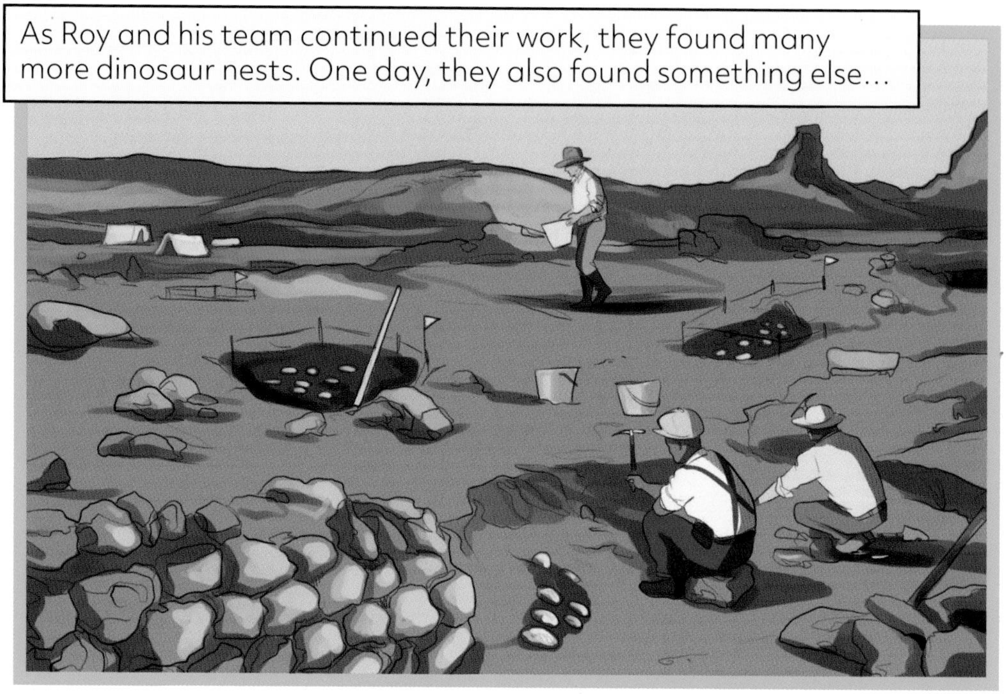
As Roy and his team continued their work, they found many more dinosaur nests. One day, they also found something else…

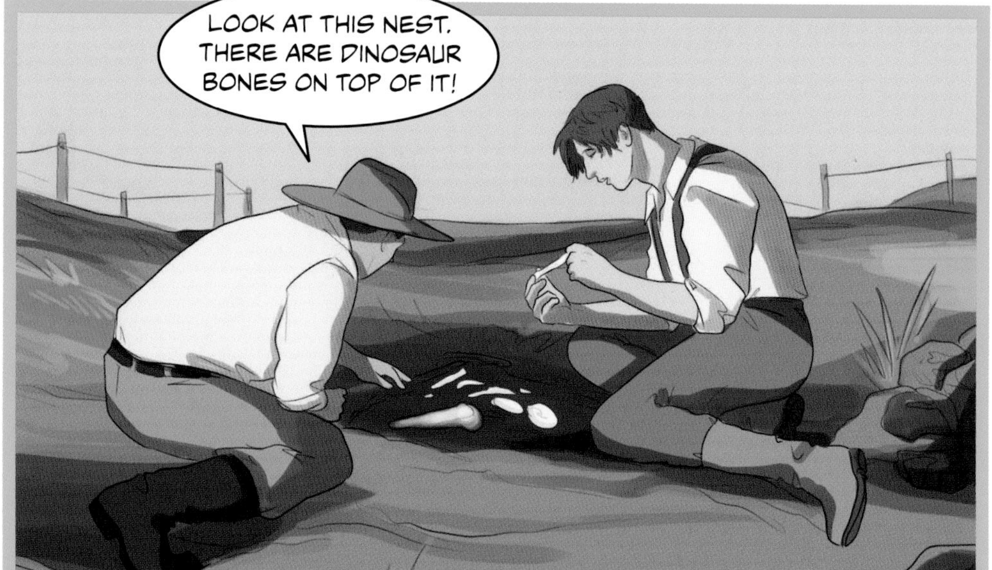
LOOK AT THIS NEST. THERE ARE DINOSAUR BONES ON TOP OF IT!

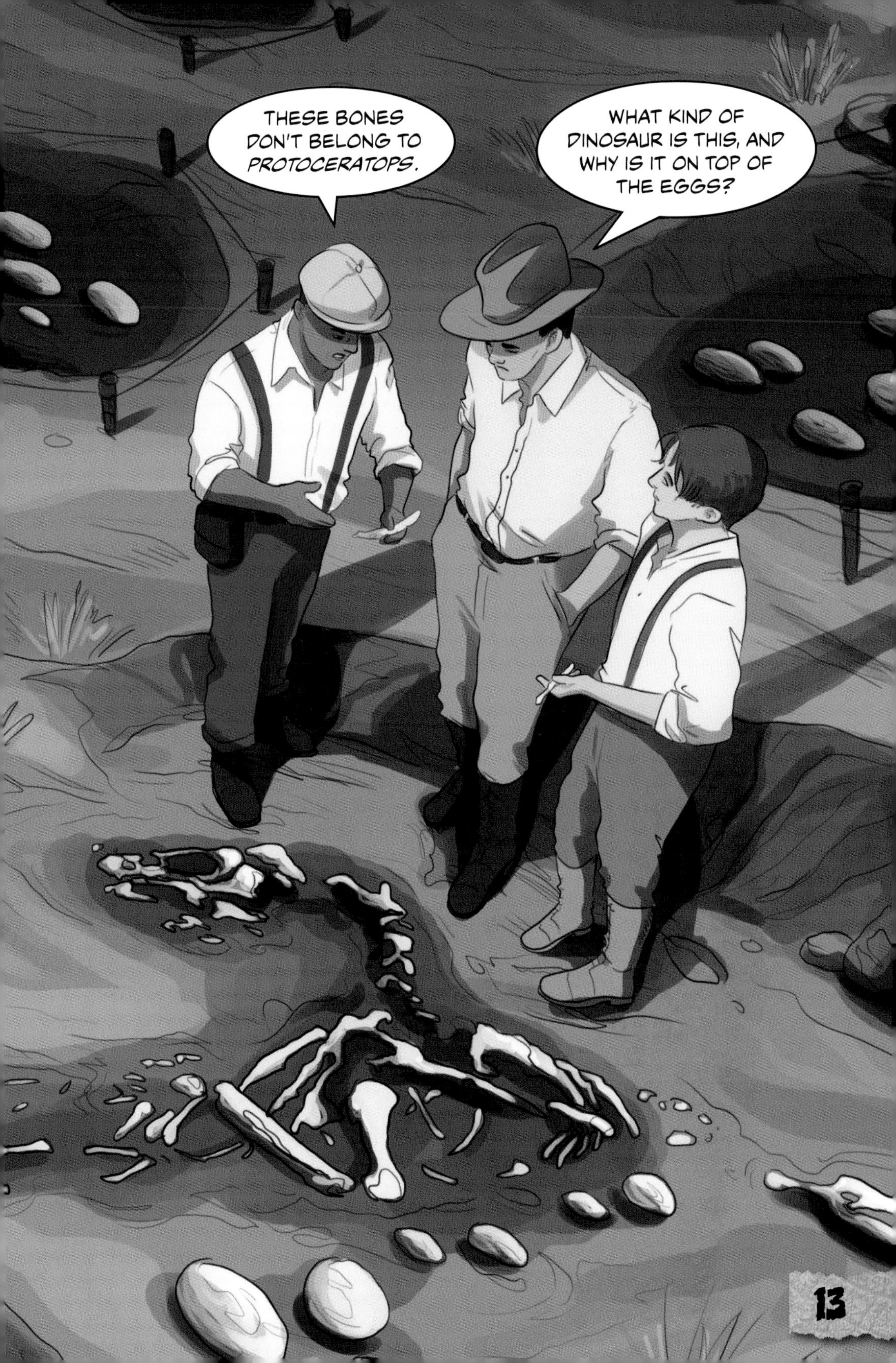
THESE BONES DON'T BELONG TO *PROTOCERATOPS*.
WHAT KIND OF DINOSAUR IS THIS, AND WHY IS IT ON TOP OF THE EGGS?

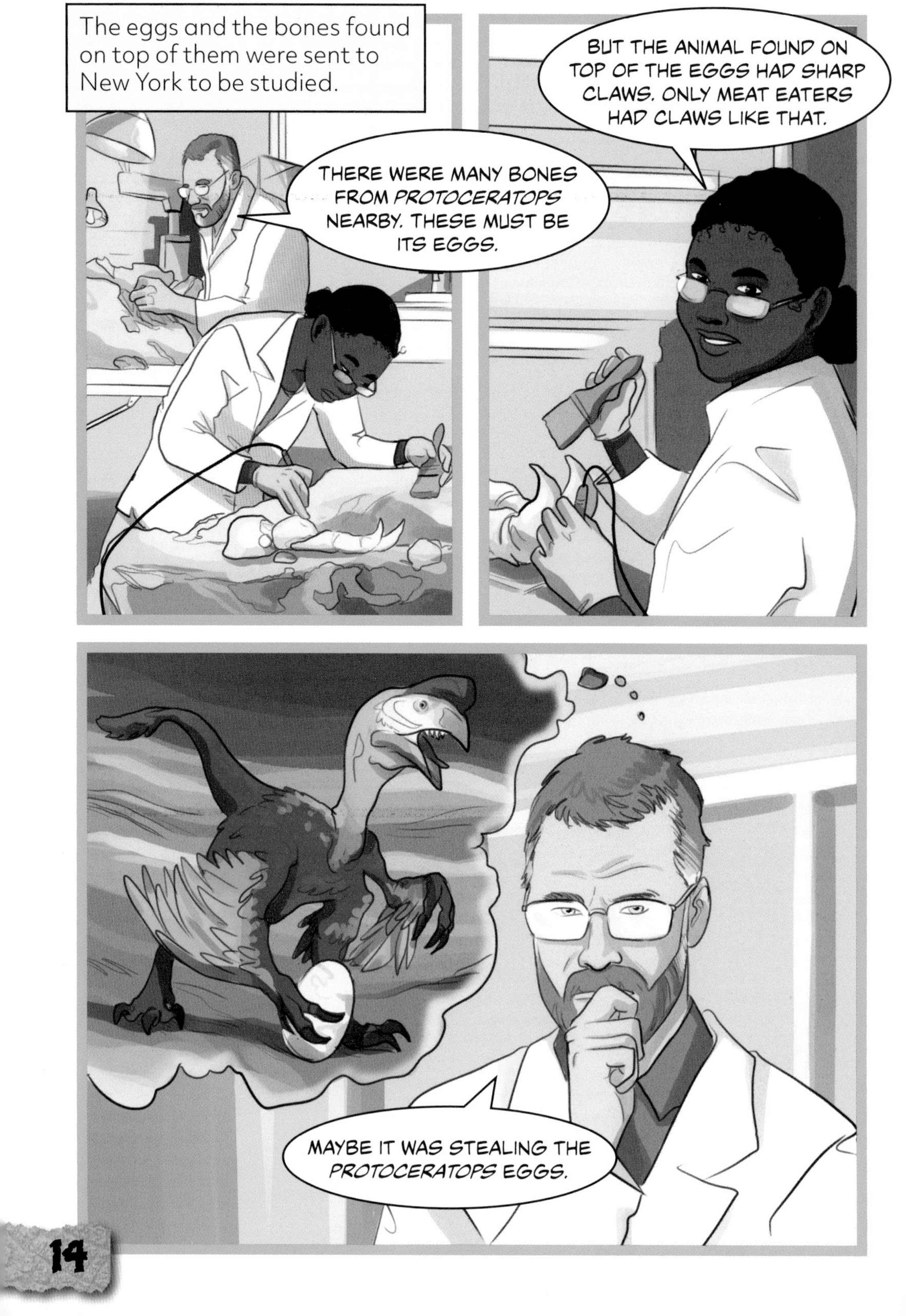
The eggs and the bones found on top of them were sent to New York to be studied.
THERE WERE MANY BONES FROM *PROTOCERATOPS* NEARBY. THESE MUST BE ITS EGGS.
BUT THE ANIMAL FOUND ON TOP OF THE EGGS HAD SHARP CLAWS. ONLY MEAT EATERS HAD CLAWS LIKE THAT.
MAYBE IT WAS STEALING THE *PROTOCERATOPS* EGGS.

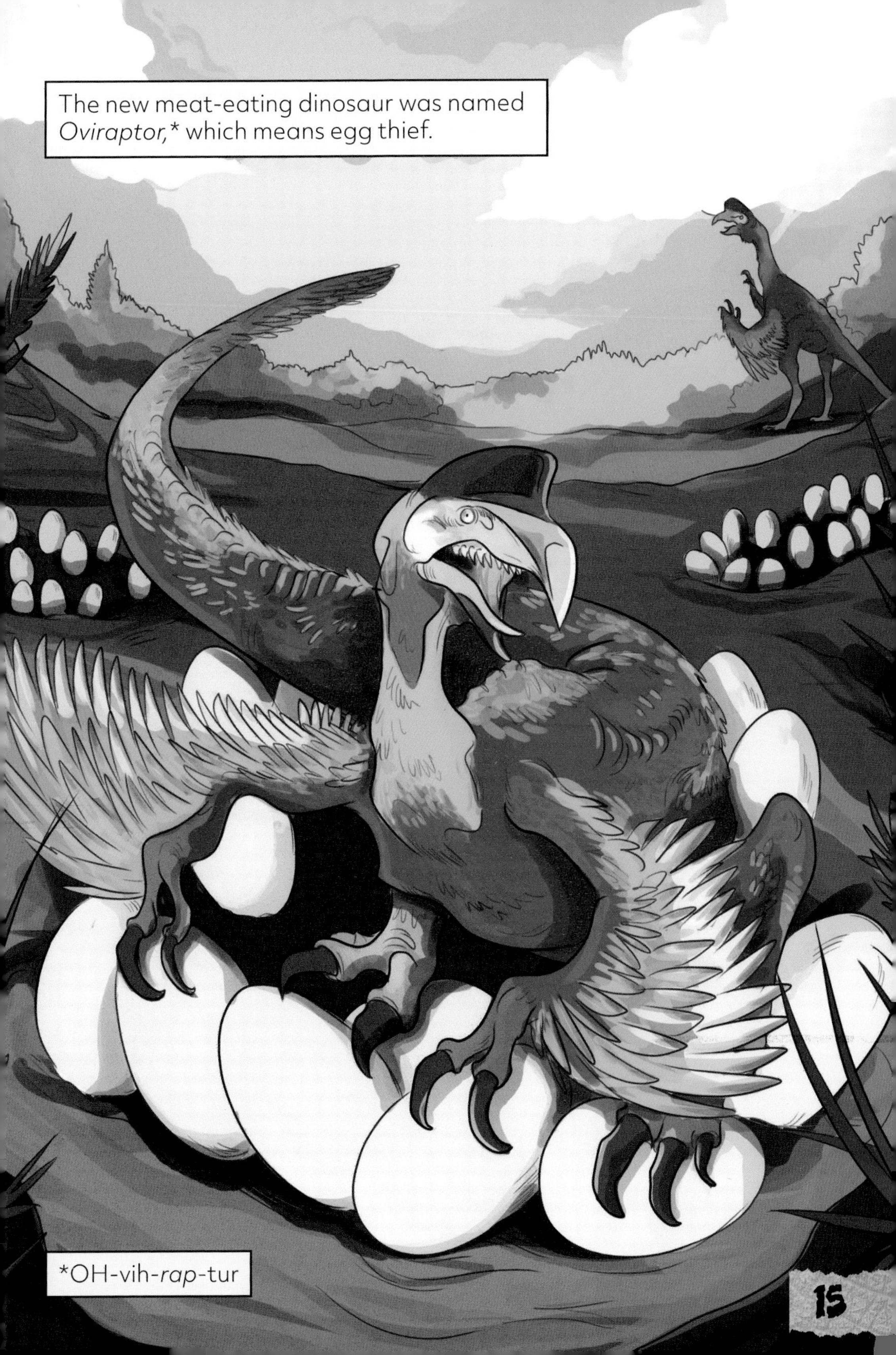
The new meat-eating dinosaur was named *Oviraptor,** which means egg thief.
*OH-vih-*rap*-tur

CHAPTER 4

A GOOD PARENT

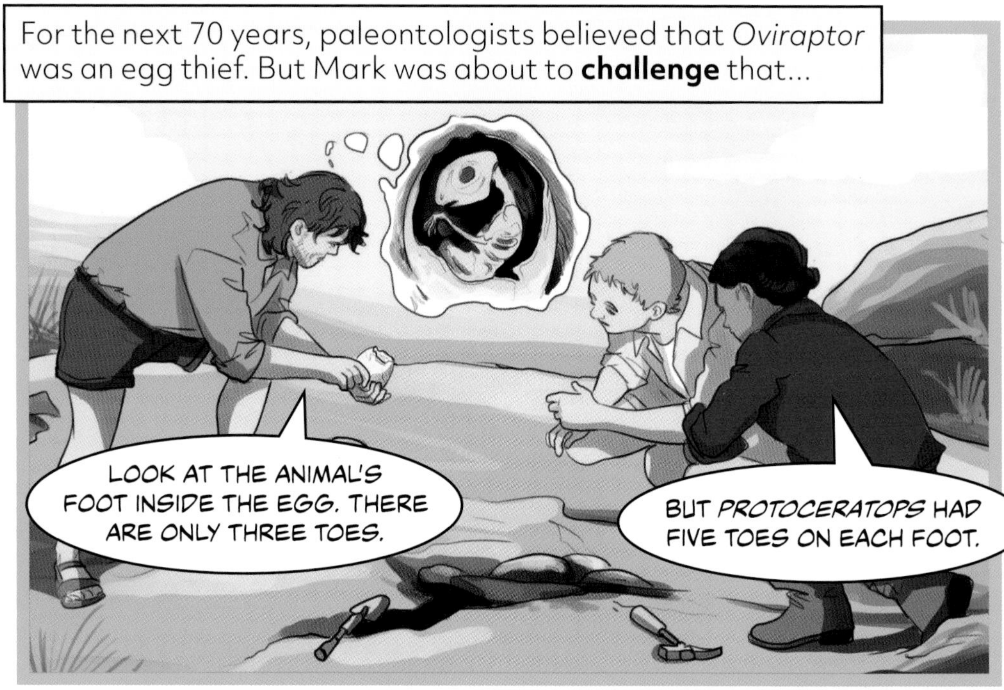
For the next 70 years, paleontologists believed that *Oviraptor* was an egg thief. But Mark was about to **challenge** that...
LOOK AT THE ANIMAL'S FOOT INSIDE THE EGG. THERE ARE ONLY THREE TOES.
BUT *PROTOCERATOPS* HAD FIVE TOES ON EACH FOOT.

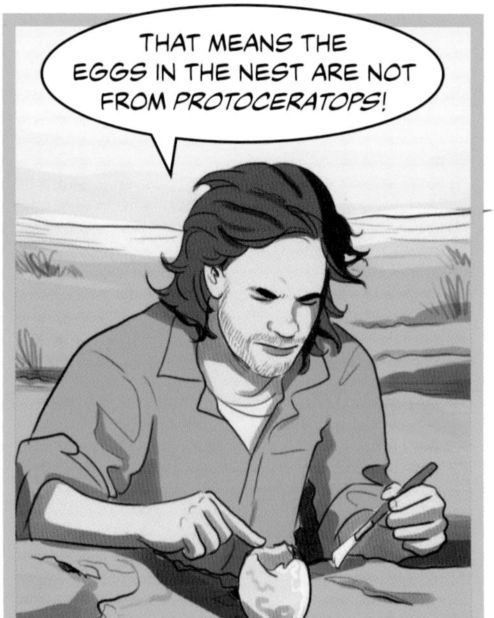
THAT MEANS THE EGGS IN THE NEST ARE NOT FROM *PROTOCERATOPS*!

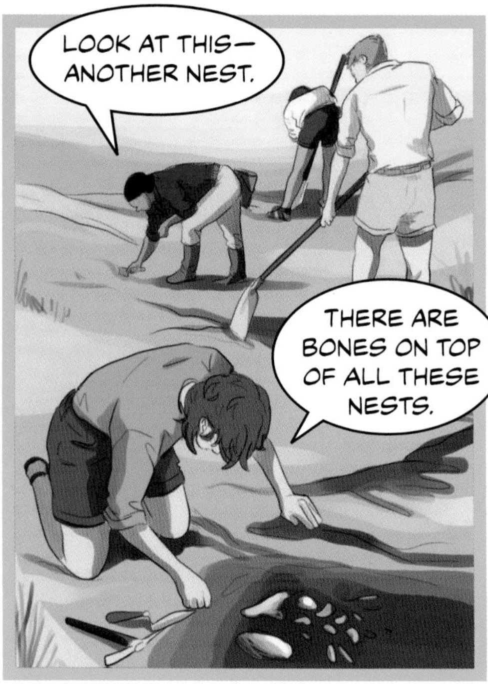
LOOK AT THIS— ANOTHER NEST.
THERE ARE BONES ON TOP OF ALL THESE NESTS.

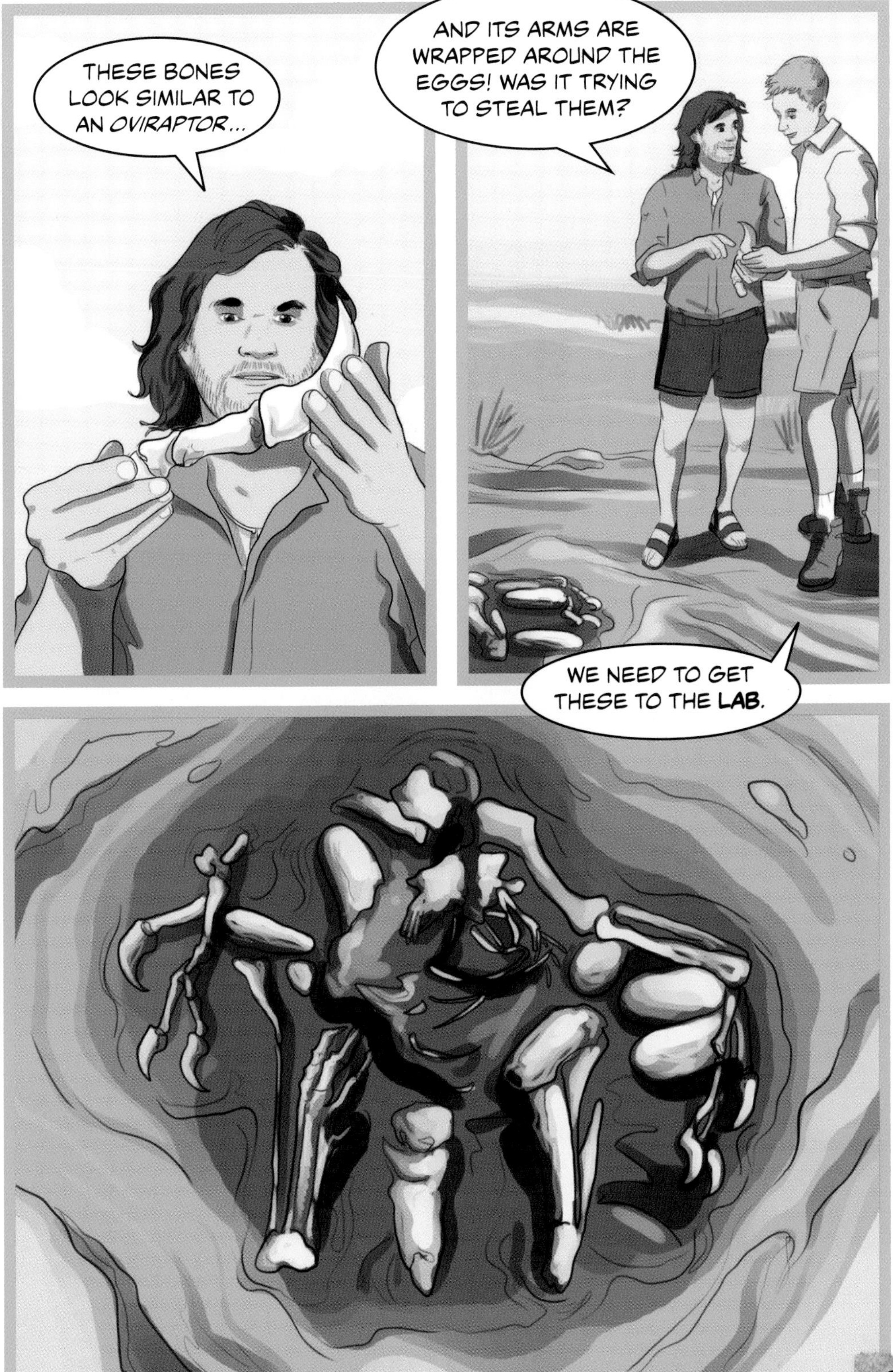
THESE BONES LOOK SIMILAR TO AN *OVIRAPTOR*...
AND ITS ARMS ARE WRAPPED AROUND THE EGGS! WAS IT TRYING TO STEAL THEM?
WE NEED TO GET THESE TO THE **LAB**.

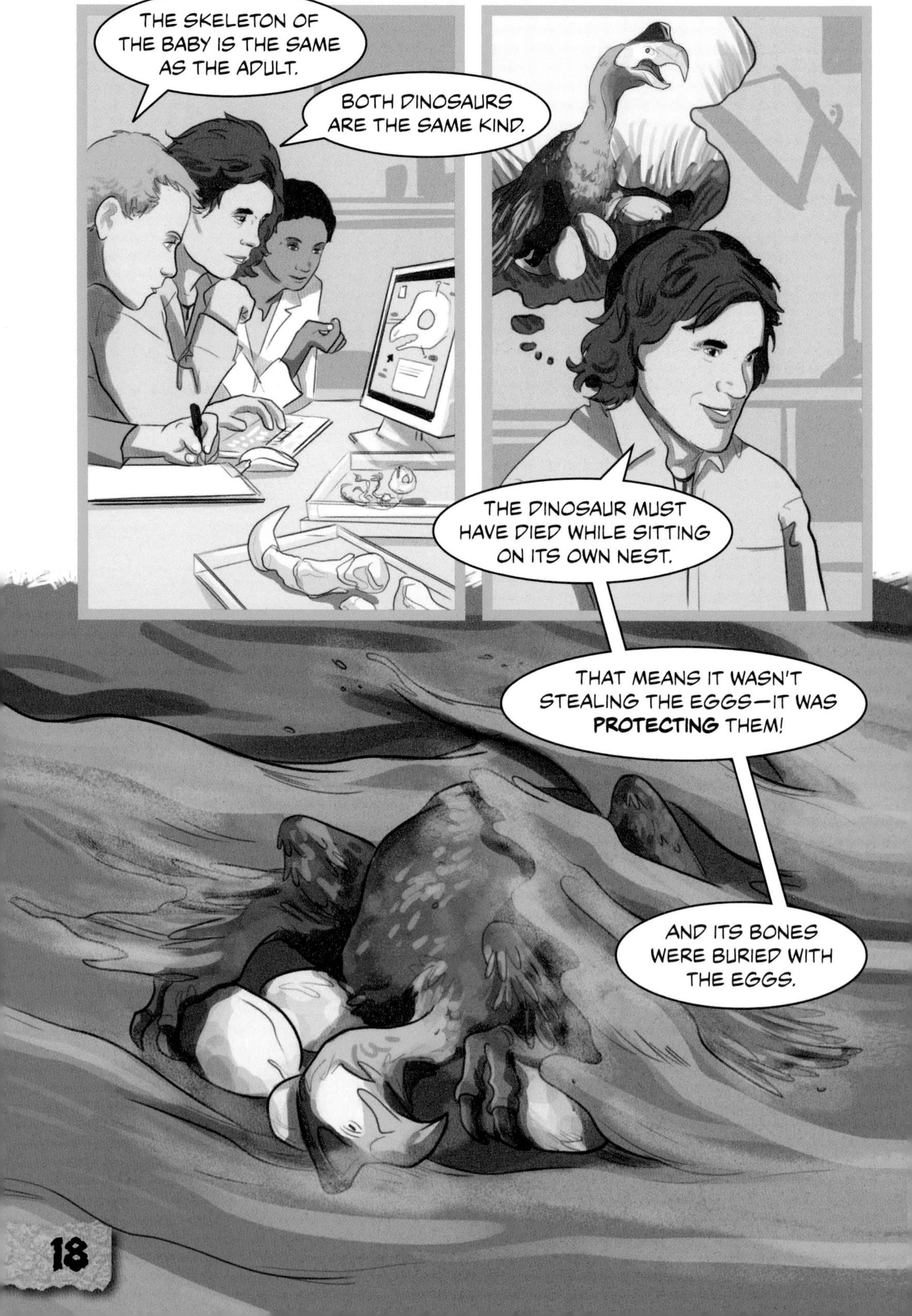
THE SKELETON OF THE BABY IS THE SAME AS THE ADULT.
BOTH DINOSAURS ARE THE SAME KIND.
THE DINOSAUR MUST HAVE DIED WHILE SITTING ON ITS OWN NEST.
THAT MEANS IT WASN'T STEALING THE EGGS—IT WAS **PROTECTING** THEM!
AND ITS BONES WERE BURIED WITH THE EGGS.

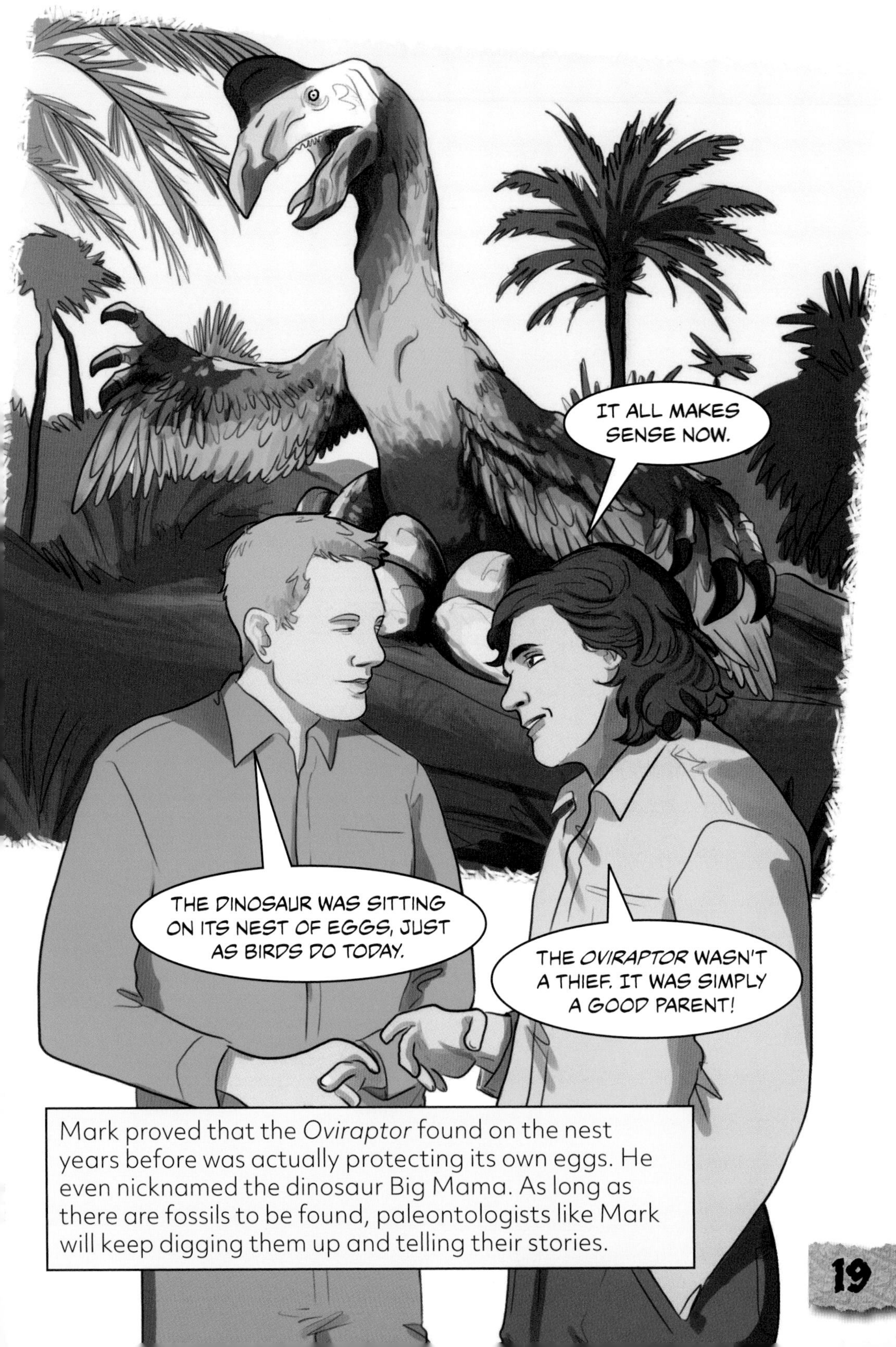
IT ALL MAKES SENSE NOW.
THE DINOSAUR WAS SITTING ON ITS NEST OF EGGS, JUST AS BIRDS DO TODAY.
THE *OVIRAPTOR* WASN'T A THIEF. IT WAS SIMPLY A GOOD PARENT!

Mark proved that the *Oviraptor* found on the nest years before was actually protecting its own eggs. He even nicknamed the dinosaur Big Mama. As long as there are fossils to be found, paleontologists like Mark will keep digging them up and telling their stories.

Who Lived with *Oviraptor*?

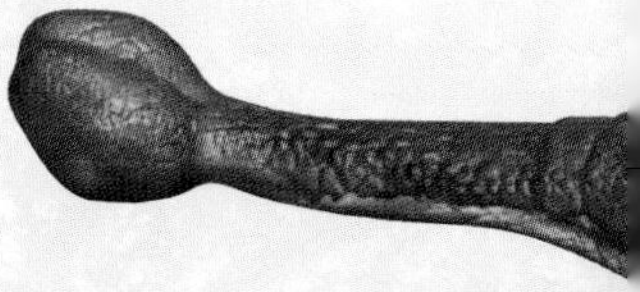

Dinosaurs lived on Earth for about 150 million years. Scientists divide the time in which the dinosaurs lived into three periods—the Triassic period (252 to 201 million years ago), the Jurassic period (201 to 145 million years ago), and the Cretaceous period (145 to 66 million years ago).

Oviraptor and *Protoceratops* lived near the end of the Cretaceous period. Both animals were about the same size—6 feet (1.8 m) long. Here are three dinosaurs that lived alongside them.

VELOCIRAPTOR

(vuh-LOSS-uh-*rap*-tur)

This meat eater was similar to *Oviraptor* in many ways. What else do we know about *Velociraptor*?

- It had long, flexible arms and powerful feet with sharp claws.
- It used its long, straight tail for balance when running and kicking.
- It was 7 ft (2 m) long.

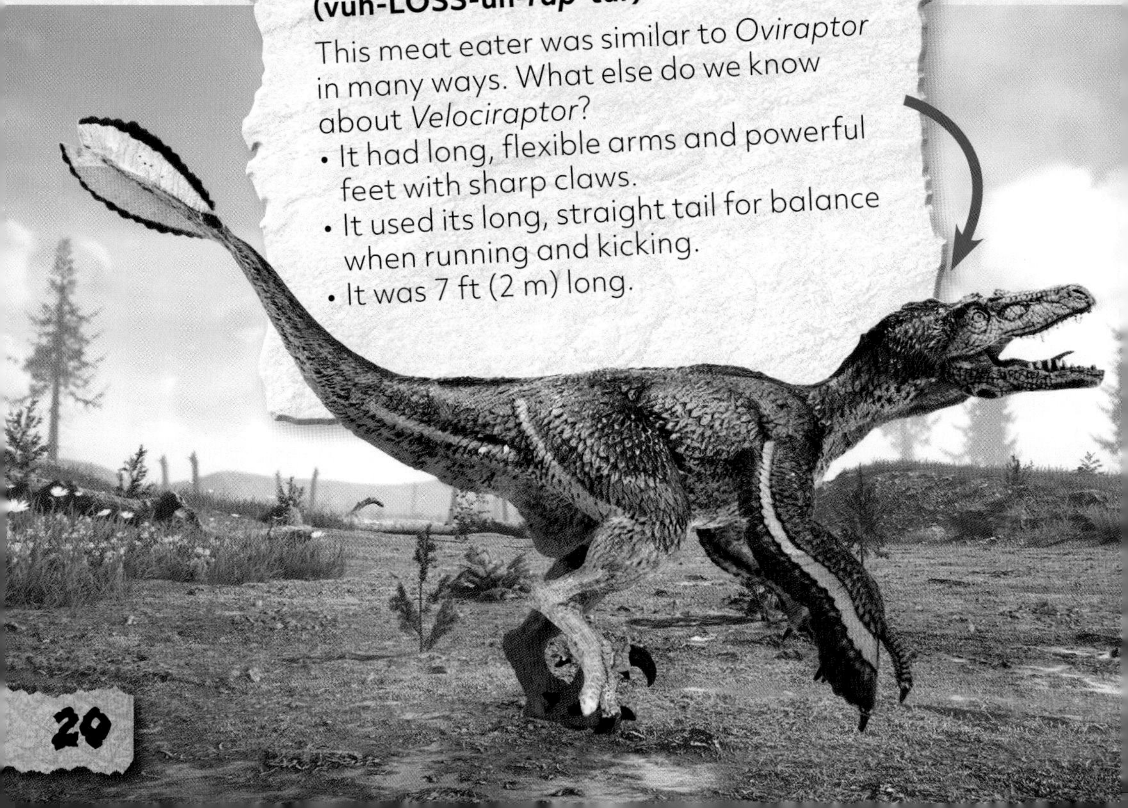

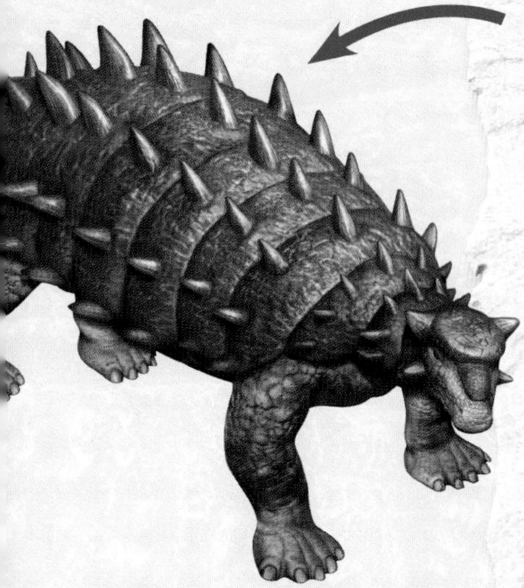

PINACOSAURUS

(pin-AH-koh-*sor*-uhss)

This plant eater belonged to a group of dinosaurs called ankylosaurs (AN-kee-luh-*sorz*). The upper part of an ankylosaur's body was covered with an armor of bony plates. What are some other facts about *Pinacosaurus*?

- Like other ankylosaurs, it had a club-shaped tail.
- It moved its tail from side to side for protection when attacked.
- It was 18 ft (5.5 m) long.

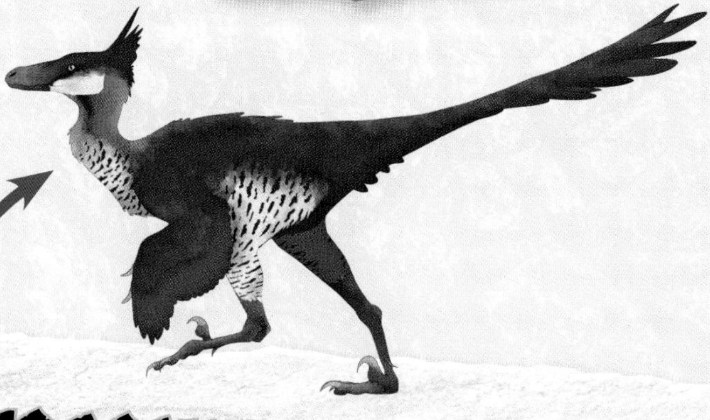

SAURORNITHOIDES

(sor-or-NIH-thoi-deez)

This meat eater probably also had a lot in common with *Oviraptor*. Its fossils are much rarer, though. What have we learned about *Saurornithoides*?

- It had a long, narrow skull similar to a bird's skull.
- It also had long, powerful arms and three-fingered hands to grab **prey**.
- It probably hunted small animals, with the help of its excellent sight and hearing.
- It was 7 ft (2 m) long.

What Is Paleontology?

Paleontology is the study of fossils, which are what is left of things that lived millions of years ago. Fossils are found in rock. Paleontologists use special tools to carefully remove the fossils from the rock so they can study them. By studying fossils, paleontologists can figure out where a plant or animal lived, what it looked like, and how it lived.

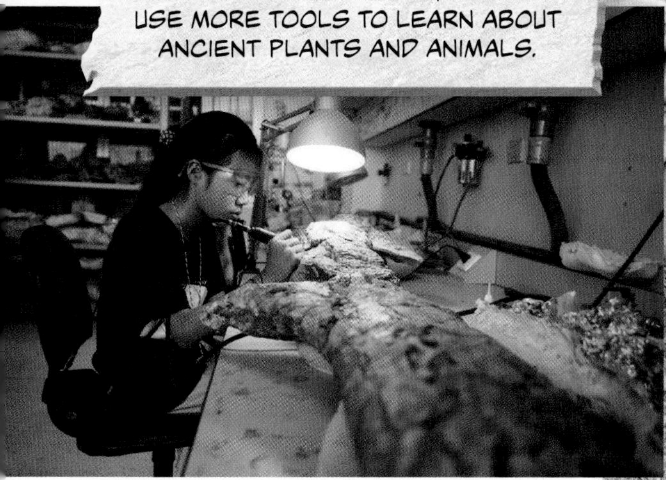

SOMETIMES PALEONTOLOGISTS STUDY FOSSILS IN LABS. THERE, THEY CAN USE MORE TOOLS TO LEARN ABOUT ANCIENT PLANTS AND ANIMALS.

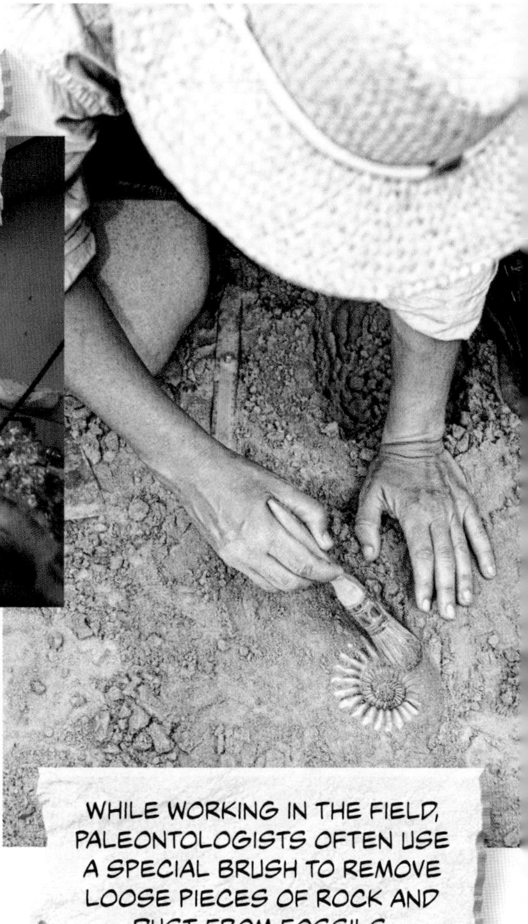

WHILE WORKING IN THE FIELD, PALEONTOLOGISTS OFTEN USE A SPECIAL BRUSH TO REMOVE LOOSE PIECES OF ROCK AND DUST FROM FOSSILS.

Fossils can show how living things changed over time, too. Paleontologists can use fossils to find out what happened to an **environment** in the past and how living things **adapted** to the changes.

Glossary

adapted changed in order to handle new conditions

challenge to question something or say that something might be wrong

environment the conditions that surround a living thing

expedition a long trip taken for a specific reason, such as exploring

fossils the hardened remains of things that lived long ago

lab short for laboratory; a place in which scientists study

paleontologist a scientist who studies fossils to find out about life in the past

prey animals that are hunted and eaten by other animals

protecting keeping something safe

remains the body or body parts of a living thing left behind after it has died

FOSSILS HELP SCIENTISTS UNDERSTAND WHAT DINOSAURS LOOKED LIKE. THEY CAN USE THIS INFORMATION TO BUILD MODELS OF THEM.

Index

Read More

Brundle, Joanna. *Dinosaurs (Discover and Learn)*. New York: Rosen Publishing, 2022.

Sabelko, Rebecca. *Oviraptor (Epic: The World of Dinosaurs)*. Minneapolis: Bellwether Media, 2021.

Taylor, Charlotte. *Digging Up Dinosaur Fossils (Dig Deep into Fossils)*. New York: Enslow Publishing, 2022.

Learn More Online

1. Go to **www.factsurfer.com** or scan the QR code below.
2. Enter "**Egg Thief**" into the search box.
3. Click on the cover of this book to see a list of websites.